by Jeff Sinclair

ACROSS CANADA

Puzzles,
Games
and
Activities
from
Sea to Sea

Scholastic Canada Ltd.

In memory of Nana and Willie —
a dream fulfilled, a promise kept
— J.S.

6 5 4 3 2 1   Printed in Canada   03 04 05 06 07

CANADA . . . it's a pretty cool place!

And we're not just talking about ice and snow!

We're talking about the second-largest country in the world. A country that is home to breathtaking snow-capped mountains, ancient rainforests, vast expanses of flowing prairie, frozen Arctic tundra, gently rolling hills and brilliant autumn woodlands.

We're talking about a place that is said to contain 1/7 of all the fresh water on the entire planet. We're talking about the place where green garbage bags, green ink and the goalie mask were all invented. Yes, we're talking about CANADA . . . our home and native land.

From Halifax to Hudson Bay, from Nunavut to Nanaimo, come join us in discovering what makes Canada one of the most exciting and diverse places you'll find anywhere on earth. From Calgary to Chicoutimi, from the Peace River to Parry Sound, come explore her character from coast to coast, and her splendour from sea to sea.

So . . . are you ready to get started on your *Across Canada* adventure? You may want to bring along a pencil and paper for some of the great games you'll be playing along the way. And you may want to pack a lunch . . . Canada is a pretty big place!

CANADA . . . cool, eh?

Canada is the world's second-largest country by land mass, covering 9 093 507 square kilometres.

The capital of Canada is Ottawa, in the province of Ontario.

In 2002, Canada's population was 31.2 million people.

The national flag of Canada, featuring a maple leaf and red and white colours, became the official flag of Canada on February 15, 1965.

The first explorer to reach Canada was John Cabot in 1497. He claimed the land for England.

Canada's 2 official languages are English and French.

Canada has close to 2 million lakes which cover almost 7.6% of the entire country.

Sir John A. Macdonald became the first prime minister when the Dominion of Canada was formed in 1867.

Canada's first commercial railway, the Champlain and St. Lawrence Railroad, began operation in 1836.

Quebec, Canada's biggest province, is almost 7 times larger than the United Kingdom.

"O Canada" was composed in 1880 by Calixa Lavallée. The original lyrics were written in French by Judge Adolphe-Basile Routhier. A century later, on July 1, 1980, "O Canada" was proclaimed the national anthem.

Canada contains 39 national parks, 50 territorial parks, over 1000 provincial parks and 850 national historic sites.

Hockey and lacrosse are Canada's national sports. Other popular sports include baseball, basketball, golf, skiing, soccer, tennis, swimming, curling and football.

YUKON

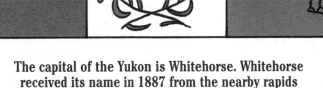

The capital of the Yukon is Whitehorse. Whitehorse received its name in 1887 from the nearby rapids on the Yukon River, where the frothing waters resemble the manes of white horses.

Jack London wrote *Call of the Wild* based on his time spent in the Yukon wilderness.

During the gold rush, an upstream trip by sternwheeler from Dawson to Whitehorse took 4 to 6 days. The trip downriver could be completed in a day and a half.

It is believed that the first people to come to Canada arrived over 10 000 years ago and first settled in the Yukon. They were the ancestors of the aboriginal people who live there today.

The Yukon Territory covers 483 450 square kilometres.

The Yukon Quest, called the toughest sled dog race in the world, is an annual 1600-kilometre endurance test between Fairbanks, Alaska and Whitehorse, Yukon.

Today, the population of the entire Yukon Territory is 29 000.

The highest mountain in Canada is Mount Logan at 5959 metres.

The portion of the Yukon above the Arctic Circle is known as "the land of the midnight sun," because the sun shines almost non-stop for 3 months during the summer. But in winter, darkness sets in and there is no sun for 3 months.

The northern lights, seen in the night skies of the Yukon, are also known as the aurora borealis.

ROADSIDE ATTRACTION →

Burwash Landing: Largest Gold Pan in the World

Before gold was discovered in 1896, Dawson was just a seasonal fishing camp. By 1898, its population had grown to 40 000, which made it the biggest Canadian city west of Winnipeg.

Chilkoot Trail

If you wanted to join the Klondike gold rush, you actually needed a TON of stuff. The Canadian government required every prospector to bring enough supplies to last one year. That's about 900 kilograms (2000 lbs.) worth of gear. And they had to haul it all up over the Chilkoot Pass. No easy feat, indeed!

GOLD PAN

FLOUR – 400 lbs.

SUGAR – 100 lbs.

BACON – 150 lbs.

HAND SAW

APRICOTS – 25 lbs.

BUTTER – 25 lbs.

PICK

SHOVEL

CANVAS SACKS – 25 lbs.

Trivia Canada: The recipe for Nanaimo bars comes from the British Columbia town of the same name.

Total Recall

Study the 20 items you would take on your Klondike expedition for ONE MINUTE, then close the book. Now get out your pencil and paper and write down as many as you can remember without looking. The person with the most correct answers gets an old box of rusty nails.

FRY PAN

MATCHES – 1 tin

KNIFE AND FORK

5/8" ROPE – 200 ft.

GALVANIZED PAIL – 14-quart

CASTILE SOAP – 5 bars

NAILS

NAILS

NAILS – 16 lbs.

HOT WAX

CANDLES

CANDLES – 1 box

COMPASS

TENT

Northwest Territories

The Northwest Territories is home to over 37 360 people, and 15 000 of them live in Yellowknife, the capital.

The economy of the territory is rooted in the mining industry: zinc, petroleum, and gold. Canada's first diamond mine went into production here in 1998.

Great Bear Lake is the eighth-largest lake in the world, while Great Slave Lake ranks as the tenth-largest. Together, they cover an area of 59 896 square kilometres.

Ancestors of the Dene people came to the Northwest Territories about 10 000 years ago. It is believed that the Inuit arrived 5000 years after that.

The provincial flower is the mountain avens.

In 1771, Samuel Hearne, a Hudson's Bay Company agent, became the first white man to visit the shores of Great Slave Lake. Matonabbee, a Yellowknife, was the leader of the Dene natives who guided him on this journey.

At one time, the Northwest Territories included all of Alberta, Saskatchewan, and the Yukon, and most of Manitoba, Ontario and Quebec!

Canada's longest river, the Mackenzie, flows from Great Slave Lake for 4241 kilometres until it drains into the Beaufort Sea. The river was named for Alexander Mackenzie, who explored it in 1789.

Yellowknife Bay, and later the city, were named after the Yellowknife band of the Chipewyan nation, who made their knife blades from copper.

In 1870, the government of Canada acquired Rupert's Land and the North-Western Territory from the Hudson's Bay Company, and renamed them the Northwest Territories.

The Northwest Territories is made up of two distinct regions: the taiga below the treeline with its boreal forests, and the tundra, a barren, mainly rocky area with stunted vegetation.

The provincial bird of the Northwest Territories is the gyrfalcon.

With the creation of Nunavut, the Northwest Territories was reduced in size from 3 426 320 square kilometres to 1 171 918 square kilometres.

N.W.T. RULES!

NORTHWEST WORD SCRAMBLE

If you think snowboarding down a snowy mountain peak is fun, give this wild Word Scramble a try. All the jumbled-up words you see here are made from words and animals on the Northwest Territories pages.

1. WSTETRHON RIRETROTSIE

2. RATEG ABER ELKA

3. EROBLA STERFOS

4. WIEFNKOLELY

5. LAGYRNOCF

6. KANEZEMCI EIRVR

7. TIAUOMNN SEVAN

8. UEMALS EARNHE

9. NEED

10. UNTRAD

11. FAUOTRBE ASE

12. MIADDNO

13. SALWRU

14. IGBNORH EPEHS

15. RCITCA OWLF

16. TRGEA ESVLA KEAL

17. XLNDREAAE CNEZAMKEI

18. AIGAT

19. S'DHOSUN AYB POANCMY

20. T.N.W. LERSU

Answers on page 44

Beastly Hink Pinks

Here are 10 humorous Hink Pinks about animals found across Canada. Hink Pinks are 2 rhyming one-syllable words like FAT CAT and SLY FLY. Getting all of these right would be a NEAT FEAT!

Answers on page 44

1 A wooden waterfowl

2 A prairie chicken would live in a . . .

3 Where a leaper sits and thinks

4 A dull crustacean

5 What the salmon got from the genie

6 A night bird in a very bad mood

7 What hogs call home

HOME SWINE HOME

8 A grizzly giving you the evil eye

9 What Bullwinkle drinks for breakfast

10 A buck deer without a mate has . . .

Nunavut

Nunavut became Canada's newest territory on April 1, 1999. Iqaluit was chosen to be its capital in 1995.

With an area of 2 million square kilometres, Nunavut contains 1/5 of all the land in Canada.

In Inuktitut, the Inuit language, Nunavut means "our land."

The land and sea mammals that make Nunavut their home have been a food source for the Arctic peoples for more than 4000 years. These mammals also provide the materials for tools, shelter and clothing.

With a population of about 6000, Iqaluit is the smallest provincial capital in Canada.

The population of Nunavut is 26 745.

The climate of Nunavut is one of harshest on earth, but the Inuit people learned how to adapt to it long ago.

50% of all the polar bears in the world live in Nunavut.

NUNAVUT IS COOL!

The Inuit name for caribou is *tuktu*.

There are over 750 000 caribou living in the Nunavut region.

Nunavut's flag contains an image of an inuksuk — a human figure made of stone. It is used to guide people across the land, or to mark important places.

Where's Polaris?

Trivia Canada: There is only one Inuktitut language, but it has more than 20 different dialects.

We now know that 50% of all the polar bears in the world live in Nunavut. Well, it looks as though most of them have come together on these two fur-filled pages. The truth is, REAL polar bears have 5 toes, so all but ONE of these hungry bears are polar bear wannabes. Can you pick Polaris out of the crowd? The first person to spot him gets a bucket of frozen fish.

Answer on page 44

Lost and Found

As you make your way across Canada, there are 20 items that you'll need to spot to complete your Lost and Found list. These assorted items have a way of showing up anywhere on any page.

Answers on page 44

So...you say you lost two bucks?..

LOST	**FOUND** on page
flying pig	_____
prospector's compass	_____
beaver holding a pencil	_____
Canada geese	_____
pink-and-blue maple leaf	_____
lump of coal	_____
lobster with one claw	_____
gushing oil well	_____
polar bear wearing sunglasses	_____
lighthouse	_____
bird perched in a tree	_____
lobster trap	_____
raven	_____
snowy owl	_____
cob of corn	_____
wristwatch	_____
Mountie's hat	_____
maple syrup buckets	_____
outline of Nova Scotia	_____
bumblebee	_____

Trivia Canada: The wettest place in Canada is Prince Rupert, B.C., with an annual precipitation of 2552 millimetres.

British Columbia

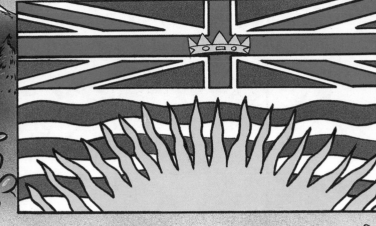

Aboriginal tribes came to the B.C. coast thousands of years ago, and developed complex societies long before the arrival of the Europeans.

In 1778, Captain James Cook anchored off the coast of Vancouver Island, and claimed it for England.

B.C.'s total area is 944 735 square kilometres.

B.C.'s ocean waters boast the world's largest octopus, scallop and sea star!

B.C. has a population of 4.1 million. That's the third highest of Canada's provinces.

Many of the Chinese-Canadians who live in Vancouver are the descendents of the thousands of Chinese people who helped build the Canadian Pacific Railway.

In 1994 The World's Tallest Totem Pole (54.94 metres) was raised in Victoria.

The ancient Haida village at Ninstints has been designated a World Heritage Site.

Abbotsford, B.C. is the Raspberry Capital of Canada, producing 15.6 million kilograms annually. That's 1/2 kilogram for every Canadian.

Vancouver Island is the largest island off the west coast of the Americas. It is also the home of B.C.'s capital, Victoria.

British Columbia has many mountain ranges, including the Rocky Mountains and the Coast Mountains.

B.C. has more varieties of plants and animals than any other province in Canada.

The oldest tree in Canada is a 1300-year-old Douglas fir that can be found in B.C.'s Stoltmann Wilderness.

KNOW YOUR CAPITALS...

The Cranberry Capital of Canada is Richmond, B.C.

Agassiz, B.C. calls itself the Corn Capital of Canada.

Born in B.C.:

Nelly Furtado, Victoria; Diana Krall, Nanaimo; Jason Priestly, Hayden Christensen, Joshua Jackson and Ross Rebagliati, Vancouver.

Swimming with the Salmon

The coho salmon are spawning and the grizzly bears are hungry. You'll need to navigate your way to the top of the page before the bears decide to put YOU on the menu. If you land on a salmon's tail, you can jump to its mouth. Land at the top of a slippery log and take a slide, Clyde.

This game can be played alone, or by several people, with one or 2 dice. You could use coins, pebbles or shells for your playing pieces.

46 47 48 49 50

33 31

34 32

35 27 29

26 28 30

14

15 13 12 11

6 9

7 8 10

15

Picture This!

Here are 7 goofy groups of pictures and letters that make up the names of Canadian cities and provinces.

If you get them all right in less than 3 minutes, blow your moose horn.

Answers on page 44

Alberta

Alberta covers an area of 661 190 square kilometres, and is almost twice as big as Japan.

Over 1/2 of Alberta, about 350 000 square kilometres, is covered by forests.

In 1754, Anthony Henday became the first European explorer to reach Alberta.

Alberta became a province on September 1, 1905, and Edmonton was chosen as its capital.

For 10 days every summer, over one million people celebrate cowboy culture at the Calgary Stampede.

KNOW YOUR CAPITALS...

Calgary is the Beef Capital of Canada.

For thousands of years, the area that is now Alberta was inhabited by many aboriginal nations, such as the Beaver, Blackfoot, Blood, Cree, Gros Ventre, Kootenay, Piegan, Sarcee and Slavey.

Born in Alberta:

Jann Arden, Calgary; Kurt Browning, Rocky Mountain House; Jill Hennessey and Michael J. Fox, Edmonton.

Over 3 million people live in Alberta.

Alberta was named for Princess Louise Caroline Alberta, the fourth daughter of Queen Victoria.

Chinooks are warm winds that blow through the Rocky Mountains and into Alberta. On January 27, 1962, the temperature in Pincher Creek, Alberta soared from -18.9°C to +3.3°C in one hour!

Alberta is responsible for 55% of Canada's oil production and over 80% of its natural gas production.

ONCE UPON A TIME, 75 MILLION YEARS AGO . . .

Alberta's exotic badlands are home to Dinosaur Provincial Park, a United Nations World Heritage Site. Over 300 dinosaur skeletons have been pulled from the area, including that of the Albertosaurus.

Peter Pond established the first fur-trading post in Alberta in 1778.

The Shape of Things

Answers on page 44

Can you recognize all of the provinces and territories just by their shapes? Some of the outlines may be upside down or sideways to make it even more challenging.

1
2
3
4
5
6
7
8
9
10
11
12
13

18

Saskatchewan

Regina is known as the home of the RCMP. The police force has trained there since 1885, when the RCMP was known as the North West Mounted Police.

Saskatchewan has a population of just over one million people.

The provincial flower is the western red lily.

Saskatchewan joined Confederation on September 1, 1905.

Before becoming Saskatchewan's capital, Regina was called Wascana, from the Cree word for "Pile of Bones." This was because of the huge quantity of buffalo bones that lay there.

Saskatchewan is the only province in Canada that doesn't have Daylight Saving Time. Clocks are set to Central Standard Time 12 months of the year.

To encourage immigration to Saskatchewan, the government offered settlers free land.

The world's most northerly sand dunes are in Athabasca Provincial Park. They reach as high as 30 metres.

Saskatchewan covers a rectangular area of 651 900 square kilometres. It has more golf courses per capita than any other province in Canada.

The name Saskatchewan comes from the Plains Cree word *kisiskatchewani*, meaning "swift flowing" river.

Born in Saskatchewan:

Leslie Nielsen, Regina; Catriona LeMay Doan, Saskatoon.

Saskatchewan produces 54% of Canada's wheat, and is nicknamed "Canada's breadbasket."

The World's Largest Moose can be seen in Moose Jaw.

The average Saskatchewan farm is about 519 hectares in area.

The waters of Little Manitou Lake are so heavy with minerals, people actually float. The lake is believed to be 3 times saltier than the ocean.

Established in 1887, Saskatchewan's Last Mountain Bird Observatory is North America's oldest bird sanctuary.

With 2540 hours of sunshine a year, Estevan, Saskatchewan is the sunniest place in Canada.

SIMPLY A-MAZE-ING

Holy Cash Crop! Kirby Kernel has to make his way down to the Gladmar grain elevator before he starts to spoil. You can show Kirby the way by marking the quickest route through the wacky wheat maze.

Solution on page 44

GO!

FINISH

What's Wrong with This Farm?

There are 12 things on this funny farm in Fillmore that just don't seem right. Your challenge is to find and remember them all before you look up the answers on page 44.

Trivia Canada: Eastend, Saskatchewan is home to "Scotty" the T-rex. Scotty is believed to be one of the most intact T-Rex skeletons ever found. He is still being excavated.

Manitoba

Manitoba has an area of 650 000 square kilometres, which is 6.5% of Canada's total.

Winnipeg is Manitoba's capital city and is home to about 60% of the province's 1.15 million people.

Upset that their land was being given to the settlers, the Métis, led by Louis Riel, started a rebellion in 1869.

KNOW YOUR CAPITALS... Portage La Prairie is known as the Strawberry Capital of Canada.

ONE BIG OLD BUG!

The World's Biggest Trilobite fossil was discovered near Churchill. It's over 445 million years old, and at 70 centimetres long, it is 70% larger than the previous record holder.

Outside of Winnipeg, at Lower Fort Garry National Historic Site, you can see the oldest still-intact trading post in North America. The fort was established in 1831.

The provincial flower is the prairie crocus and the provincial bird is the great grey owl.

Lord Selkirk established the first agricultural settlement in the Red River Valley in 1812.

Baldy Mountain is Manitoba's highest point at 831 metres.

Manitoba has the greatest difference between summer and winter temperatures. In the summer it has a high of 40° Celsius, and in the winter a low of -40° Celsius. That's a difference of 80°!

Manitoba is known as the "land of 100 000 lakes."

Born in Manitoba:

Terry Fox, Anna Paquin and Chantal Kreviazuk, Winnipeg; Loreena McKennitt, Morden; Susan Aglukark, Churchill.

THE GREAT CANADIAN TRIVIA TEST

PART I

1. Who wrote *Call of the Wild*, based on his Yukon experiences?
   a) Jack London   b) Jack the Ripper   c) Jack England

2. Name the provincial flower of the Northwest Territories.
   a) mountain violet   b) Mountain Dew   c) mountain avens

3. Nunavut contains what percentage of all the land in Canada?
   a) 1/2 minus 1/4   b) 1/3   c) 1/5

4. Warm winds in Alberta winters are known as what?
   a) Canucks   b) chinooks   c) a welcome relief

5. The average Saskatchewan farm is how many hectares in area?
   a) 195   b) 915 591 159   c) 519

6. Which province has the sunniest spot in Canada?
   a) Saskatchewan   b) Manitoba   c) the one with the smallest clouds

7. In 1867, who became Canada's first prime minister?
   a) Sir Donald McDonald   b) Sir Ronald McDonald   c) Sir John A. Macdonald

8. Who was the first person to chart the area that is now B.C.?
   a) Capt. James Cook   b) Capt. James T. Kirk   c) West Coast Wally

9. Drumheller, Alberta is home to what famous dinosaur?
   a) Stegosaurus   b) Albertosaurus   c) Barney

10. Manitoba goes by the name "Land of _____."
    a) 100 000 Lakes   b) 50 000 Puddles   c) Monster Mosquitoes

Answers on page 44

Across Canada CROSSWORD

ACROSS

1. Corn Capital of Canada
4. Canada's biggest province
5. 1/5 of Canada
6. Gold was discovered in Dawson City, _____
8. Albertosaurus lived here
11. Warm Alberta wind
12. The capital of Ontario
13. A national symbol of Canada
14. Eighth-largest lake in the world
17. 80% of the people in Quebec live in the areas along the _____
18. Canada's top farmed fish

DOWN

2. Manitoba provincial bird, _____ _____ owl
3. First Prime Minister in 1867
6. A colourful utensil to use with a fork
7. 54% of Canada's wheat is grown here
9. Inuit word for caribou
10. Some of the first New Brunswick inhabitants
11. Canada is _____
15. Province named for fourth daughter of Queen Victoria, Princess Louise Caroline _____
16. World's second-largest country by land mass

Answers on page 44 & 45

24

Ontario

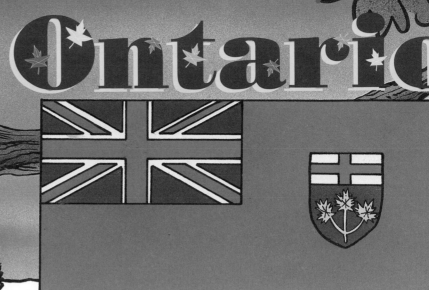

The word Ontario is Iroquois for "sparkling water." It's a good name for a province that contains over 250 000 lakes!

Ontario covers 1 068 580 square kilometres. That is almost twice as big as Texas, the second-biggest state in the U.S.

The capital of Ontario is Toronto. It is also the largest city in Canada with over 4.6 million people in its metropolitan area.

The Iroquois and Algonquin nations are the descendants of Ontario's first inhabitants who arrived over 10 000 years ago.

In 1610, Henry Hudson became the first European to set foot on the shores of Hudson Bay, which was named for him.

Ontario is home to almost 12 million people, about 1/3 of Canada's population.

Ontario produces about 40% of all the goods that are made in Canada.

Born in Ontario:

Bryan Adams, Kingston; Dan Aykroyd and Alanis Morissette, Ottawa; Neve Campbell, Guelph; Amanda Marshall, Toronto; Martin Short, Hamilton; Shania Twain, Windsor.

The World's Longest (and still growing) Gum Wrapper Chain is in Waterdown, Ontario.

In 1867 Ontario was one of the first provinces to join the Confederation of Canada.

KNOW YOUR CAPITALS...

Talk about diversity! About 60% of new immigrants to Canada settle in Ontario, and over 100 different languages are spoken within its borders.

The Tomato Capital of Canada is Leamington, Ontario.

Frankford, Ontario is the Wild Turkey Capital of Canada.

The smallest jail in North America is in Rodney, Ontario.

With 14 kilometres of pure white sand, Wasaga Beach is said to be the longest freshwater beach in the world.

Lake Superior is the largest freshwater lake in the world.

WEIRD WILDERNESS

The animals in Algonquin Park have come together for some fireside fun. It's pencil and paper time again as you try to spot all the weird things that are going on here. There are 13 items you'll need to find. Why 13? . . . Because it's WEIRD!

Answers on page 45

Coast-to-Coast Alphabet Adventure

Fill in the missing letters to discover the people, places and things that make up Canada.

Each one is either mentioned or can be seen somewhere in the book. Then take all the letters that are circled and unscramble them to learn the hidden message.

Answers on page 45

1. B _ _ _ _ (A) Y
2. _ H I _ H O _ S _
3. P _ I C _ E _ _ R _ _ S L _ N _
4. _ _ L _ (O) N
5. G R _ _ D _ _ N K S
6. M _ _ _ E _ E _ F
7. _ _ S _ A T (O) _ _ W _ N
8. _ R E _ (O) _ R _ C T _ _
9. L _ _ S T _ _
10. B _ I _ I _ H (C) O _ _ M _ _ A

11. J O _ N _ M _ _ _ _ (N) _ L _
12. _ A B R _ _ _ _
13. _ U _ S (O) _ B _ _
14. _ _ O N _ I _ E
15. _ O _ A S C _ _ I (O)
16. B _ _ V _ _
17. _ (A) C _ O (O) S E
18. _ U _ _ E _
19. A (L) _ _ _ _ O _ A U _ _ _
20. G _ _ (O) Z Z L Y _ E A _

Hidden Message Answer:

◯◯◯◯◯◯   ◯◯   ◯◯◯◯

Trivia Canada: The Atlantic salmon is the most important fish species farmed in Canada, and 2/3 of it is farmed in B.C. on the *Pacific* coast!

Quebec

Quebec is Canada's largest province, with an area of 1 667 926 square kilometres. This is over 3 times the size of France.

The Canadian Shield covers most of Quebec, and has rocks that are 900 million years old — some of the oldest on earth.

Canada's top inventor, Reginald Fessenden, held over 500 different patents. He was born in East Bolton, Quebec, in 1866.

Montreal is Quebec's largest city with over 3.38 million people in its metropolitan area. This makes it the world's second largest French-speaking city, after Paris.

Quebec produces 70% of the world's maple syrup.

Some 80% of Quebec's population lives in areas along the St. Lawrence River.

The snowy owl is Quebec's provincial bird.

Every February, Quebec City hosts Carnaval, their famous winter festival.

The province's name comes from the Algonquin word *kebek,* which means "where the river narrows."

Jacques Cartier and his crew were the first Europeans to spend a winter in Quebec. That was in 1535.

The population of Quebec is now over 7 million.

Born in Quebec:

Celine Dion, Charlemagne; Marc Garneau and Norm McDonald, Quebec City; Caroline Rhea, Montreal; Jacques Villeneuve, St-Jean-sur-Richelieu.

The capital of Quebec is Quebec City. It is the only walled city in North America. The walls run more than 4 kilometres around the town.

Aboriginal people settled in the St. Lawrence Valley over 6000 years ago. Today Quebec is still home to 70 000 aboriginal people.

The St. Lawrence River, which links the Atlantic Ocean and the Great Lakes, is 1000 kilometres long.

Spot the Differences
Riding Down the Richelieu River

Time to get out your pencil and a piece of birchbark to write on. The picture on the right has missing, added or changed items in it. See if you can spot the 10 differences before the traders pass by on their journey downriver. After you're done, you can colour in both scenes. Try doing one with autumn colours and one with a winter feel.

Answers on page 45

Maritime Hinkie Pinkies

Remember Beastly Hink Pinks? Now try doing 10 Hinkie Pinkies that are made up of two 2-syllable rhyming words. They are all about things you might find on the east coast of Canada.

Answers on page 45

1 A criminal crustacean is a ...

2 Where the skipper lives when he comes ashore

3 What you get when your sucker drops on the beach

4 A game bird that is always happy is a ...

5 A man who spies a romping river mammal is an ...

6 A fuzzy raccoon late for work is in a ...

7 What makes you seasick?

8 A seagull with 8 pens and a calculator is a ...

9 A flat-tailed creature with a temperature has ...

10 A fisherman who gives away some of his catch is ...

Trivia Canada: King's College in Windsor, Nova Scotia, is Canada's oldest university. It was founded in 1789.

New Brunswick

The Bay of Fundy is a popular feeding ground for many types of whales, including the humpback, the finback, the pilot and the right whale, as well as the orca or killer whale. There are also pods of dolphins and porpoises and large seal herds.

85% of New Brunswick is covered in forests.

The Miramichi River has some of the best salmon fishing in the world.

The Malecite and Mi'kmaq peoples and their descendants have lived on the shores of New Brunswick for centuries.

New Brunswick covers an area of 73 500 square kilometres. That's about 0.7% of Canada's total land mass.

With 125 000 people in its metropolitan area, Saint John is New Brunswick's largest city.

KNOW YOUR CAPITALS...

Inkerman, New Brunswick is known as the UFO Capital of Canada.

756 000 people call New Brunswick home.

The World's Largest Axe was presented to the town of Nackawic, New Brunswick. The steel axe is 18.28 metres long, 7 metres wide, and weighs 7 tonnes. It was estimated that it would take a 140-tonne lumberjack to swing it!

Fredericton is the provincial capital.

NEW BRUNSWICK IS AWESOME!

At Magnetic Hill, cars that are put in neutral appear to be pulled up the hill in defiance of gravity.

The provincial flower is the purple violet.

The Bay of Fundy is famous for the highest tides in the world. In a 24-hour period, the ocean levels can change up to 15 metres.

New Brunswick is Canada's only officially bilingual province, and 33% of its inhabitants are francophones. That is the largest percentage outside of Quebec.

The world's longest covered bridge was completed in Hartland in 1899. It is 390 metres long.

New Brunswick joined the Dominion of Canada on July 1, 1867.

Fredericton's Favourite Word Search

As the wind and waves whip against the New Brunswick shoreline, try to search out all the words before high tide.

Solution on page 45

Word list:

- ATLANTIC OCEAN
- BAY OF FUNDY
- CHALEUR (Bay)
- COD
- FLOUNDER
- FORESTS
- FREDERICTON
- ST. LAWRENCE
- HUMPBACK
- JACQUES CARTIER
- LOBSTER
- MALECITE
- MI'KMAQ
- MONCTON
- MOUNT CARLETON
- MUSSELS
- NEW BRUNSWICK
- NORTHUMBERLAND (Strait)
- SEAGULL
- SAINT JOHN

O	D	G	C	B	K	R	A	Q	T	U	K				
N	A	H	F	D	C	O	D	S	K	C	B				
E	O	T	I	E	I	K	L	B	A	H	A				
E	E	R	L	J	W	M	O	B	Y	A	Y				
C	R	C	T	A	S	R	P	Z	P	L	J				
N	F	T	L	H	N	M	E	Y	O	E	I				
E	O	F	M	F	U	T	G	D	H	U	N	J	B	J	A
R	P	R	N	H	R	M	I	X	N	R	O	M	A	A	N
W	Q	E	C	D	B	D	B	C	K	U	I	J	Y	C	O
A	B	D	R	S	W	E	W	E	O	M	O	H	O	Q	T
L	A	E	T	U	E	F	C	C	R	C	G	L	F	U	E
T	W	R	V	E	N	V	H	G	L	L	E	L	F	E	L
S	A	I	N	T	J	O	H	N	L	L	A	A	U	S	R
N	Y	C	Z	I	J	S	O	U	U	A	B	N	N	C	A
O	X	T	K	C	L	T	D	H	G	F	M	N	D	A	C
T	L	O	R	E	S	S	T	P	A	E	Z	A	Y	R	T
C	M	N	S	L	Y	E	L	Q	E	G	C	B	E	T	N
N	P	S	N	A	X	R	E	T	S	B	O	L	A	I	U
O	U	O	Q	M	C	O	M	D	R	F	B	W	G	E	O
M	I	K	M	A	Q	F	A	B	E	S	T	U	H	R	M

Nova Scotia

The population of Nova Scotia is about 950 000.

Nova Scotia has an area of 55 491 square kilometres.

Nova Scotia has more than 5400 lakes, and its coastline is scattered with more than 3800 small islands.

ROADSIDE ATTRACTION →

The World's Largest Mastodon makes the town of Stewiacke famous.

The province has about 10 500 kilometres of winding and twisting shoreline. That's longer than the Trans-Canada Highway — the longest national highway in the world.

Nova Scotia is Latin for New Scotland, but the province is also known as "Canada's Ocean Playground."

Evidence from an archeological site at Debert shows that people have lived in Nova Scotia for at least 10 000 years.

Halifax is Nova Scotia's capital, as well as the largest city in the province with some 117 000 residents.

Born in Nova Scotia:
Anne Murray, Springhill;
Sarah McLachlan, Halifax.

Sable Island, off the coast of Nova Scotia, is known as the "graveyard of the Atlantic." Over 350 shipwrecks have been recorded there. The island is also home to several hundred wild horses.

 Oxford, Nova Scotia is the Blueberry Capital of Canada.

In 1605, Samuel de Champlain established Port Royale. It was one of the first permanent European settlements.

Nova Scotia has 150 lighthouses — the most in Canada!

The largest documented lobster was caught in Nova Scotia in 1977. It weighed 9.3 kilograms and was 1.26 metres long.

Lurking in the Weeds and Waves

Take a gander (and we don't mean Newfoundland) at all the aquatic activity off the shores of Nova Scotia. Hidden among the weeds and waves are 10 items that have no place being in the waters of the Bay of Fundy. Once you have spotted all 10, take some time to colour in this awesome sea scene!

Answers on page 45

Food for Thought

Here's a yummy game sure to puzzle your palate. Each picture clue below is a popular food in a certain province or territory. It's up to all you budding chefs to figure out what goes where. Get all of them correct and reward yourself with a bag of Beaver Bark Chips!

Answers on page 45

1. Nanaimo Bars

2. Lunenburg Lobster Bisque

3. Pancakes with Maple Syrup

4. Big and Beefy 32 oz. Steak

5. Cod Chowder

6. Memories of Winnipeg Creamy Cheesecake

7. Wild Turkey

8. Weyburn Wheat Bread

9. Summerside Spuds

10. Caribou Stew

Trivia Canada: Al Gross, who was born in Toronto, invented the walkie-talkie in 1938 and the telephone pager in 1949.

Prince Edward Island

Prince Edward Island joined the Dominion of Canada on July 1, 1873.

Prince Edward Island is Canada's smallest province in both size (5660 square kilometres) and population (139 000).

50% of its land is under cultivation.

KNOW YOUR CAPITALS...

There are over 800 kilometres of beaches along the island's shores.

P.E.I. has been nicknamed "The Garden Island."

Prince Edward Island is the Potato Capital of Canada.

The Mi'kmaq people have lived on the island for at least 2500 years. They called it *Abegweit,* which means "cradled by the waves."

Over 1.8 million people visit Prince Edward Island each year.

Lucy Maud Montgomery, who wrote the famous Anne novels, was born in Cavendish, Prince Edward Island.

Confederation Bridge now joins P.E.I. to the rest of Canada. A marvel of engineering, it stretches almost 13 kilometres across the Northumberland Strait.

Anne of Green Gables has been translated into 15 languages worldwide.

The island is known as "The Birthplace of Canada," and "The Cradle of Confederation," because Charlottetown hosted the meetings that led to Canadian Confederation.

The capital of P.E.I. is Charlottetown.

P.E.I. ROCKS!

Automobiles were banned on P.E.I. from 1908 until 1911. It wasn't until 1919 that they were allowed on the roads every day of the week.

Newfoundland and Labrador

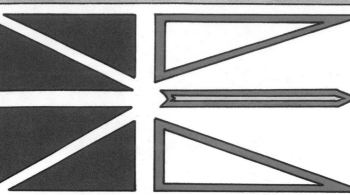

Thorfinn Karlsefni, a Norseman, built the first European settlement at L'Anse aux Meadows, Newfoundland, in 1003.

Cape Spear, Newfoundland, is the most easterly point of North America. It is also a National Historic Site and home of Newfoundland's oldest standing lighthouse.

The island of Newfoundland is 112 000 square kilometres, and including Labrador, it has an area of 405 720 square kilometres.

People on the east coast of the island are closer to Ireland than they are to Saskatchewan.

Much of the island and Labrador are covered by thick forests of balsam fir and black spruce.

The Torngat Mountains are the highest in Labrador. The name comes from the Inuit word for spirits, *turngait*. According to Inuit legend, this is the place where the spirit world overlaps our own.

The Grand Banks is one of the largest and richest resource areas in the world. It is famous for its valuable fish stocks and petroleum reserves.

Newfoundland joined Canadian Confederation on March 31, 1949, making it Canada's newest province.

The population of Newfoundland and Labrador is over 530 000.

Today, 4 aboriginal groups live in the province: the Inuit, the Innu, the Métis and the Mi'kmaq.

ONE MEAN CITY!
Compared to other Canadian cities, St. John's has the most foggy days (121) and the most days of freezing precipitation per year (38), plus the greatest average annual wind speed (24 kilometres per hour).

St. John's is the capital of Newfoundland and Labrador. It is also the province's largest city, with about 175 000 residents.

There are no snakes, skunks, or poison ivy on the island of Newfoundland.

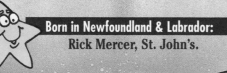

Born in Newfoundland & Labrador:
Rick Mercer, St. John's.

THE GREAT CANADIAN TRIVIA TEST

PART II

1. The Bay of Fundy is famous for the highest _____ on earth.
a) taxes   b) tides   c) telephone poles

2. What Ontario lake is the largest freshwater lake in the world?
a) Lake Mammoth   b) Lake Inferior   c) Lake Superior

3. 80% of Quebec's population lives near what river?
a) St. Florence   b) St. Lawrence   c) St. Bernard

4. Prince Edward Island grows the most _____ in Canada.
a) potatoes   b) extra toes   c) tomatoes

5. Some of the most productive fishing grounds in the world lie off the shores of Newfoundland. What is this area called?
a) Great Banks   b) Grand Banks   c) Piggy Banks

6. What does the Iroquois word "Ontario" mean?
a) sparkling water   b) filtered water   c) filthy water

7. Nova Scotia is known to Canadians as what?
a) Canada's Ocean Playground   b) Lobster World   c) The Crabby Capital of Canada

8. 85% of New Brunswick is covered in what?
a) 6 metres of water   b) forests   c) squirrels looking for trouble

9. Cod chowder is a popular food in which part of Canada?
a) Newfoundland   b) British Cod-umbia   c) the fishy part

10. 50% of all the land on P.E.I. is under _____?
a) 1 metre tall   b) arrest   c) cultivation

Answers on page 45

Labrador Labyrinth

START

And you thought Kirby Kernel had it tough. Now it's time to help Luba the Labrador retriever scramble back to her doghouse. Watch out for slippery rocks and swooping seagulls as you try to cross this puppy!

Solution on page 46

FINISH

LUBA

LUBA

43

Answers

Northwest Word Scramble

1) Northwest Territories
2) Great Bear Lake
3) boreal forests
4) Yellowknife
5) gyrfalcon
6) Mackenzie River
7) mountain avens
8) Samuel Hearne
9) Dene
10) tundra
11) Beaufort Sea
12) diamonds
13) walrus
14) bighorn sheep
15) Arctic wolf
16) Great Slave Lake
17) Alexander Mackenzie
18) taiga
19) Hudson's Bay Company
20) N.W.T. rules

Beastly Hink Pinks

1) Spruce Goose
2) Grouse House
3) Frog Log
4) Drab Crab
5) Fish Wish
6) Foul Owl
7) Pigs Digs
8) Bear Stare/Glare
9) Moose Juice
10) No Doe

Where's Polaris?

Polaris is the bear wearing the hot pink bib on page 11.

Lost and Found

flying pig – 21
prospector's compass – 5
beaver holding a pencil – 46
Canada geese – 1

pink and blue maple leaf – 23
lump of coal – 16
lobster with one claw – 38
gushing oil well – 17
polar bear wearing sunglasses – 11
lighthouse – 42
bird perched in a tree – 15, 26
lobster trap – 33
raven – 3
snowy owl – 29
cob of corn – 13
wristwatch – 12, 36
Mountie's hat – 16, 19
maple syrup buckets – 30, 31
outline of Nova Scotia – 18
bumblebee – 16

Picture This!

1) British Columbia
2) Winnipeg
3) Saskatchewan
4) Red Deer
5) Ontario, Canada
6) Quebec City, Quebec
7) Halifax

The Shape of Things

1) New Brunswick
2) Saskatchewan
3) Nunavut
4) Northwest Territories
5) Alberta
6) Newfoundland and Labrador
7) Yukon
8) Prince Edward Island
9) Quebec
10) Nova Scotia
11) Manitoba
12) British Columbia
13) Ontario

Simply A-Maze-ing

What's Wrong with This Farm?

1) mixed-up weathervane
2) fire in silo
3) flying pig
4) both moon and sun in sky
5) doorknob in wrong place
6) green cloud
7) cow with one horn
8) bird with glasses
9) flat tire on tractor
10) fish out of water
11) hose is cut
12) pitchfork is bent (and it's not good to run with one, either!)

The Great Canadian Trivia Test – Part I

1) a 2) c 3) c 4) b 5) c 6) a
7) c 8) a 9) b 10) a

Across Canada Crossword

ACROSS
1. Agassiz
4. Quebec
5. Nunavut
6. Yukon
8. Drumheller
11. chinook
12. Toronto
13. maple leaf
14. Great Bear
17. St. Lawrence River
18. Atlantic salmon

DOWN
2. great grey
3. John A. Macdonald
6. Yellowknife
7. Saskatchewan
9. tuktu
10. Mi'kmaq
11. cool
15. Alberta
16. Canada

Weird Wilderness

1) Birch leaves are heart-shaped
2) Raccoon has two tails
3) Bear is wearing sunglasses
4) Bear is toasting marshmallow
   with his paw
5) Frog is blowing bubble gum
6) Propane lantern has electrical cord
7) Beaver is holding cellphone
8) Two moons are in the sky
9) Fish is fishing
10) Snake has two heads
11) Tent peg is out of ground
12) Bird is flying upside down
13) Tent has satellite dish

Coast-to-Coast Alphabet Adventure

1. blue jay
2. Whitehorse
3. Prince Edward Island
4. salmon
5. Grand Banks
6. maple leaf
7. Saskatchewan
8. Fredericton
9. lobster
10. British Columbia
11. John A. Macdonald
12. Labrador
13. Hudson Bay
14. Klondike
15. Nova Scotia
16. beaver
17. lacrosse
18. Quebec
19. Albertosaurus
20. grizzly bear

Hidden Message Answer:
CANADA IS COOL

Spot the Differences
Riding Down the Richelieu River

1) Maple syrup pail is missing
2) Earmuffs are missing
   from beaver
3) Emblem on canoe has changed
4) Trader's paddle blade is missing
5) Feathers on bird's head have changed
6) Beaver in canoe has lost his hat
7) Snowflakes are falling
8) More rocks are in water
9) Beaver's cut log is shorter
10) Trader's hat is black

Maritime Hinkie Pinkies

1) Lobster Mobster
2) Sailor Trailer
3) Sandy Candy
4) Pleasant Pheasant
5) Otter Spotter
6) Furry Hurry
7) Ocean Motion
8) Nerdy Birdy
9) Beaver Fever
10) Sharing Herring

Fredericton's Favourite Word Search

Lurking in the Weeds and Waves

1) wristwatch on barnacle rock
2) bottle in kelp weeds
3) pencil on rocks
4) push-pin on salmon's tail
5) fish has book for fin
6) shoe in kelp weeds
7) tire by lobster
8) crab's shell is coffee mug
9) telephone and cord above cod
10) sword in kelp

Food for Thought

1) British Columbia
2) Nova Scotia
3) Quebec
4) Alberta
5) Newfoundland and Labrador
6) Manitoba
7) Ontario
8) Saskatchewan
9) Prince Edward Island
10) Nunavut

The Great Canadian Trivia Test – Part II

1) b 2) c 3) b 4) a 5) b 6) a
7) a 8) b 9) a 10) c

Labrador Labyrinth

ABOUT THE AUTHOR

Jeff Sinclair was born in Toronto, Ontario on April Fool's Day (no joke). From his home studio just outside Vancouver, B.C., he illustrates dozens of humorous children's books that are sold all over the world.

When Jeff is not busy putting pen to paper, he can be found feeding hungry Japanese koi in his backyard pond, perfecting his already beautiful golf swing or going out in search of Canada in his RV, nicknamed "The Magic Bus."

Jeff lives with his wife Karen, son Brennan and daughter Conner, proud Canadians one and all.